One Day My Sister Disappeared

a memoir

Random House | New York

CHRISTINE ORBAN

One Day My Sister Disappeared

TRANSLATED BY

Gwen Bolkonsky

Copyright © 2004 by Christine Orban

All rights reserved under International and Pan-American Copyright Conventions. Published in the United States by Random House, an imprint of The Random House Publishing Group, a division of Random House, Inc., New York, and simultaneously in Canada by Random House of Canada Limited, Toronto.

RANDOM HOUSE and colophon are registered trademarks of Random House, Inc.

This work was originally published in French as *L'âme soeur*, copyright © 1998 by Éditions Albin Michel S.A.

Library of Congress Cataloging-in-Publication Data

Orban, Christine.
[Ame sœur. English]
One day my sister disappeared / Christine Orban; translated by Gwen Bolkonsky
p.   cm.
ISBN 0-375-50802-3
1. Orban, Christine—Family. 2. Authors, French—20th century—Family relationships. 3. Brothers and sisters—Death. I. Title.

PQ2675.R33Z464 2004
843'.914—dc22   2003058702

Printed in the United States of America on acid-free paper

Random House website address: www.atrandom.com

987654321

FIRST EDITION

Book design by Barbara M. Bachman

For Maco's children
and for all who loved her

—

If you were here,
I would have no need to write.

One Day My Sister Disappeared

I'm searching for Maco's beautiful face, her hair streaked with sunlight. I look inside my head, where all is hopeless confusion. I'm hunting for the words. I need them to re-create that gleam in her dark eyes, as if she were always on the verge of bursting into laughter. The words are my only hope now. Otherwise I will never see my little sister again and our childhood will disappear forever with her.

Death hands friendship back to the friend. My friend is gone, but not our friendship. I'm still here, weighed down by love, memories, stories I want to tell her. Life goes on, even though she's no longer here.

Her name was Corinne. I called her Ma Co, two words. *Ma* means "my" in French and *Co* is short for Corinne. In time *Ma* and *Co* were joined to form a new name. According to my parents, I rebaptized my sister.

Anxiously I watched her royal arrival in a baby carriage of white muslin. Who was this come to disturb my reign? Would she take my place or would she be a new friend? Was she a doll? I wanted to make sure. I climbed up on a stool, scissors in hand. I aimed for Maco's tiny fingernails and with one stroke cut open the tips of her thumb and forefinger. Maco screamed, staining her small white sheet with blood. But now I knew. Maco wasn't a brand-new plastic doll. I had a little sister.

Every night her loss haunts me.

Happiness vanished as suddenly as the flight of a bird. Had I really been happy? I've often blamed myself for frantically searching everywhere for what I had right next to me all the time.

I never dreamed of calling our relationship a friendship. I would have had to invent a new word, a word all our own. Friends were other people whom one had to charm. We didn't need them.

One night, without warning, Maco disappeared. A few short hours after she told me she was going to have a baby. The next day I was no longer able to hear her. I never would again. She was gone in a few seconds. After a phone conversation, in the midst of happiness, at the beginning of a new pregnancy. My sister became my sister spirit. Without warning she left me weighed down with memories, sole guardian of our secrets big and small, with this language we had invented for ourselves that only we understood, a profusion of secret words that reassured us that we belonged to the same tribe.

Today Maco is buried in the Ben m'sik cemetery, where I can never return. Still, I go to meet her, to talk about her, to discuss her in the present tense, to impose order on the chaos of my memories, to go beyond the tricks I play on myself sometimes in order to believe that she is still there, that I can still be happy for a moment, can still think of something other than her, my little sister.

O*n the white wooden* desk in our room there was a plastic globe of the world, lit from inside.

The world is blue, swallowed up by the sea.

We were born in that part of North Africa that looks out onto the Atlantic and the Azores. We live "there," Maco used to say, pointing to a far corner of the globe, off by three continents.

"There" was red earth under the sun, waves that broke just in front of the house, and the call of the muezzin at sunset. "There" was the scent of mint tea, and Aida, our nurse, who gave us our bath in the evening. "There" was a horse named Kidnapping who whinnied as a sign of welcome. As soon as I entered his stall, he would turn me around and, with his muzzle, go through my pockets looking for sugar. Kidnapping terrified Maco. I pulled at her little hand, the fingers all stiff, to get her to stroke his soft muzzle. She nick-named him Velvet Nose, but that didn't help her get over her fear. Was it the animal's size, the ringing sound of his shod hooves on the cobblestones, or the smell of the stables? I don't know. But she became my accomplice when it came to raising our two cats, Pussycat-Purr and Cindy, whom we hid under the bed when John Bull, the wild boar, and Eagle, the dog, tore up the garden.

We spent weekends at Katouat, in the house where our father stayed when he went hunting. There we dis-covered colors that were different from those at home—green and red especially—and other distractions.

There our refuge was not a wicker cabin or a shell-filled grotto, as at the beach house, but a tree, an old welcoming oak, with steps hollowed out from the bark. High up in the tree, each of us had chosen a branch as her house.

Katouat was also mule rides on saddles of braided straw that tore us to shreds and death-defying descents down the mountain on wobbling bicycles whose tires were nearly flat. One of our greatest joys was hunting scorpions. We had become extremely deft from our practice of catching crabs. Maco and I divided up the tasks. I immobilized the creature by seizing it behind the claws, while she, armed with a pair of scissors, cut off the end of the tail, where the poison was stored. Knowing where to find the scorpions was a game with few surprises; they would turn up under each sixth or seventh stone. Our harvest was not a heartless slaughter. We always spared the mothers and the babies and our catch enabled us to continue our "observations." The poor black and yellow scorpions, cut into sections, were placed under the microscope until the day our father caught us returning home from a hunt, bag of scorpions in hand. He threw them into the fire. I remember the whistling sound the roasting scorpions made and the smell of burning plastic.

Katouat was also piles of partridge, quail, and wild boar killed during hunts that were responsible for our lifelong disgust for blood and the smell of blood. It was there that we found John Bull, the wild boar who had been miraculously saved. He was no bigger than a hand when he was given to us. John Bull drank his milk from our dolls' bottle. Even though he was a boy, we knotted a pink ribbon around his neck.

With my little sister's help, I used to train our German pointer, fresh from obedience school, at the end

of a tether, taking him through a whole series of jumps as though he were a horse at a horse show. On May 18, 1968, a memorable day, the hunting dog, with our two dolls strapped to his back, jumped a yard high. Thank God our father, surprised that Eagle was so exhausted, never suspected that we had transformed his purebred hunting dog into a circus animal. Maco applauded.

That was the high point of the year. As for what was happening on the barricades in Paris, we knew nothing. We would learn about it later.

In *our house* on the Atlantic coast, our neighbors on the inland side were farmers; on the shore side they were fishermen.

One night, in a silence broken only by the sound of the waves, Mama woke us up. For the first time ever, a man was walking on the moon. It was July 1969. It would be a few years before I left. Why did I think about my departure with such a mixture of fear and curiosity that particular night?

Because going to Paris was like going to the moon.

Maco and I, sitting on the cold gray slate floor of the veranda, backs against our parents' shins, watched Neil Armstrong's first awkward steps with astonishment. In the garden we looked at the moon through the telescope, so near and so far away.

Even if I were offered a seat in a rocket going to the

moon, I would never go, but you would consider it, Maco informed me.

I hugged her tight. I knew what she was thinking about: the mythic city that was a dream for me, a nightmare for her. She hated asphalt, traffic jams, gray skies. She preferred to catch shrimp by scraping her net along the seaweed that clung to the rock.

I liked to fish too, especially in order to feed our cats. Every time we came home, Cindy and Pussycat-Purr were waiting for our little plastic bucket, which they overturned with a quick swipe of the paw. They would crunch on the live shrimp as well as the many-hued little rockfish we found in nearby puddles.

Our great excitement was night fishing. After dinner we waited for night to fall. Then, armed with spades and acetylene torches that our father had prepared in the garage, we would set out. I loved the smell of the gray stone of the torches as it burned and the fishes' surprise when we shone our light into their faces, and coming home, the game bags slung over our shoulders, full of the smell of the sea and the squishing sound of rubber boots full of water, while each of us exaggerated our adventures. But it was true that my father really did catch a conger eel and it was true that

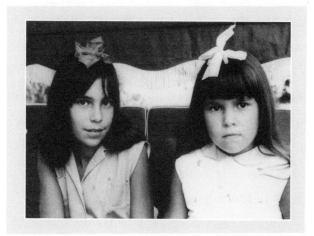

Maco and I suddenly found ourselves up to our necks in water in the midst of a shoal of mullet. One evening my father really did spear an angelfish, a fish as flat as a skate, and more than a yard long. The next day all the neighbors lined up to see the fish.

One evening, coming home from one of our expeditions, Maco said to me, "You know, Chris, I'm sure you can't fish like this in the Seine. Think about it. . . ."

The more I thought about it, the more sure I was that when the moment came, Maco would be strong enough to be willing to tear herself away from her universe.

Very early on we began to live, she and I, haunted by the fact of our coming separation. We were four years apart and there was no French university in the country where we lived. Unless we gave up any idea of studying and fished for rockfish for the rest of our lives, we had no choice. One day we would have to leave behind all that we loved. We grew up with this fear, this sword hanging over our heads.

"After you graduate, you're going away, Chris?" And she would count on her little fingers how many years we had left together.

I tried to reassure her. "You'll join me very soon. I'll

get everything ready. A little house for the two of us,· and if you come before you graduate, you can get your diploma in Paris. I'll come with you."

She didn't respond to that, but said, "In Paris, people are always in a hurry. They never have any time, Chris. . . ."

We had plenty of time, too much time. And the people around us were rich only in time, which they offered us with carefree generosity. The long days did not come to an end until the red sun, a few yards from us, sank into the ocean. Then nothing. Nothing but the backs of the fishermen who, seated cross-legged in front of the house, gazed at the horizon. Good-bye to the sun. The even expanse of the sky. The flat sea. The light breeze. And silence. How could I explain to my little sister that life would drive us from this paradise?

Often, seated in the shadow of the cave lined with shells, I would escape by reading. The first time I fell in love, it was with a character in a novel.

Maco preferred Vasco, our fourteen-year-old neighbor. Maco always preferred reality to daydreams. She preferred a real person sitting beside her on the beach to an imaginary hero.

I preferred words to reality. Words in books describe us better than we can do it ourselves. I loved the words of the Little Prince: "For me you are just a little boy like a hundred thousand other little boys. I don't need you. And you don't need me either. I'm nothing but a fox for you, just like a hundred thousand other foxes. But if you tame me, we'll need each other. For me, you'll be unique in all the world and I'll be unique in all the world for you."

This story lulled us throughout our childhood. Rereading it now, I can still hear the inflections of our mother's soft voice. I see myself again with Maco, knees drawn up to her chest, feet tucked under her nightgown, listening to my mother and hoping that the story would never end. But all stories come to an end and one looks for others. I'm angry with myself for not knowing how to hold back time and remain in the world of childhood.

We *went to sleep soothed* by the sound of the waves crashing on the rocks beneath our window. I saw only the sky, the stars, and the moon changing places. Heaven was all around us. I heard the sea. But I could not see her until she reappeared in the morning. Unless the white waves turned phosphorescent during the night.

Aida slept below. She spoke only Arabic. Our parents lived at the end of the garden, down the path studded with stones that hurt our feet.

When Mama's story was finished, we were allowed to say good night to Nounours, Pimprenelle, and Nicolas on television. Belphegor, the phantom of the Louvre, rebroadcast late in the evening, frightened us. Then we would go up to our room to sit at the back of the closet under a cloud of petticoats where we had built our dolls' house. That's where they invited one another over for dinner.

After the Barbie dolls came Bella dolls, big babies with long eyelashes. The Barbie dolls inspired unconscious thoughts of growing up. Isn't that what dolls who look like grown-up women are for? We lent them our secret language, which no one but us understood.

The dolls had moods. Maco's was unhappily married and turned to me for help. Francine, my small brunette doll with jointed legs, used to listen to Maco's too blond Barbie whose legs didn't bend but who could talk.

Later we asked Father Christmas (whom we no longer believed in) for husbands for our dolls. Two Ken dolls arrived. We were intimidated by these "man objects." They were ridiculous. Indecent. We rebelled and the Ken dolls remained in the ski outfits they were wearing when they arrived.

One day Maco, who was braver than I, insisted, "It's hot. We should undress the men." Then she asked me, "Have you ever seen a boy naked?"

I shook my head emphatically.

"What do you think it's like? Is it frightening?"

Maco and I counted to three and together we pulled the too tight underpants off the Ken dolls. But dolls, like angels, have no sex organs.

Shortly after we stripped our male dolls, the sky fell on us. Adelina, our Italian grandmother, died. With her went her unforgettable accent and her mistakes in French, which we loved to make fun of.

What was death if it meant Mama no longer spoke to us? We tried to understand why she remained so long in her room behind closed shutters.

One night we placed a bath towel on the floor and went to sleep. Pressed up against her door, we hoped that the next morning, tripping over us, she would notice us and explain why, as Aida had so bluntly informed us, our grandmother wasn't coming back.

Maco began to cry, convinced that it was her fault. Adelina was phobic about dairy products, particularly cheese. The night before she died, our grandmother had taken off her shoes. Maco, on all fours under the table, had crumbled Roquefort into her shoes.

I believed that if I wished for it with all my heart, she would come back. I said my prayers. I even invented some. I called her. But she did not come back.

Was it because I didn't wish for it with all my heart?

When Mama came out of her room at last, Maco and I, hand in hand, asked her if little girls could die too. "Little girls never die," she replied. Her lie made us far more afraid.

You can't hide the truth for long.

I *loved being a child* so much that I never wanted to grow up. The day of my first Communion, I felt sad because my white dress made me think of a wedding dress. But Maco already saw herself in a white gauze veil and wanted to know which saint to pray to for larger breasts, while I hunched my shoulders to hide mine and bent my knees in all the class photos.

When Maco was three, I helped her make mud pies, which we decorated with geranium petals. I kneaded the mud and offered them to our father to taste. That was a big risk. Maco was in love with her papa. One day, in spite of all the trouble she had gone to, he got tired of playing the gourmet and chased me away, sending me back to the age of reason. Maco could only follow.

At that time I knew only that *reason* was a bad and harsh-sounding word. I wasn't mistaken. My father's annoyance revealed a fateful dividing line: childish games are no longer acceptable when one is seven, but when one is three, one can still marry one's papa.

We felt sad and took refuge in the willow cabin at the end of the garden. Our home. A way to show them we weren't grown-up. That we weren't ready to leave the world of our dolls Liz and Claudia, or the shell-filled grotto or the oak at Katouat, our second homes.

Could we sleep there, in one of our two houses?

No.

The world of grown-ups begins by introducing itself to children with that word: no.

No, Kidnapping the horse cannot live in the garden.

No, John Bull the wild boar cannot live in your room.

No, you cannot sleep on the beach or in the grotto or the hut or light bonfires.

I hated the word *no*. But Maco learned to make fun of it before I did.

I *covered the walls* of our room with short quotations, which, from seeing them so often, we learned by heart. They were chosen by a special method that depended on what was painful at the moment.

I chose them. Maco was not one to read between the lines. She was more likely to get warmth and understanding from her friends. But once in a while one of my quotes struck a chord and she would recopy it in her pretty handwriting, remembering the upstrokes and downstrokes of the letters just as I had taught her, and she would stick it next to her bed.

Words were our paintings. That was not always to Maco's taste; she preferred posters. I resisted. I sacrificed poor Julie Andrews in *The Sound of Music*, removing the poster to make room for more quotes, while

Maco sang "Do, a Deer" and "Climb Every Mountain" to try and change my mind. Only Elvis won out. Poor Elvis, Colt .45 in hand, wedged between a quote from Proust warning us against friendship, which, he said, made us imagine that we were not hopelessly alone, and another by Freud: No one can take on my burden, it is my cross to bear, I have to bear it, and God knows my back is becoming quite bent.

We suspected, Maco and I, that Freud could not have been as close to his brothers and sisters as we were or he would not have invented psychoanalysis.

We were proud and happy to think we had felt, even for a moment, the same things as certain writers whom we admired.

The quotes placed end to end formed a long sea serpent. Soon there were so many of them, there was no longer room on our walls. So we copied them into our diaries, which we bought at the corner store on our way to school. We chose them for their flowered covers and for the little padlocks that protected our harmless secrets.

I scribbled every evening, Maco not as often. We left our keys lying about as though we hoped that people around us would read our cries for help. Maco read my diary in secret. Did she want to make sure that I wasn't hiding anything from her? That's not what the diary was for. On the contrary, I wrote it in order to understand my own secrets. Maco was too young to know that. So was I. One begins by living weighed down by thoughts whose meanings escape us. Later I understood them, though they still made me suffer.

When Maco had had enough of seeing me bent over my books, she would suggest a change of pace with our favorite game. We each had at least a hundred shells, carefully numbered and cataloged. The game consisted of trading our mother-of-pearl or spotted coffee bean shells (which were as big as an egg) as we sat cross-legged, facing each other, taking care not to be cheated.

One day Maco said to me: Could shell trading be a profession?

Maco was happier than I was. She had more of a talent for happiness. She didn't idealize friendship or dream of the perfect friend with devoted spaniel eyes. She fled from unhappiness instead of seeking it out. Maco didn't like to waste her time. She moved fast.

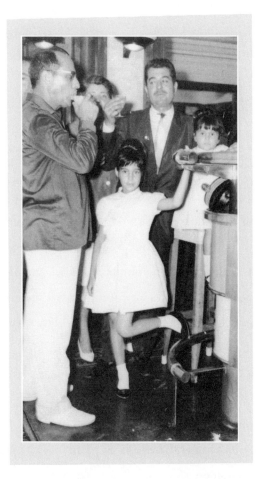

When she was still a small child, the corner grocer nicknamed her Madame Fissa Fissa. *"Fissa, fissa,"* she would say to him, "Quick, quick," when she sneaked into his shop during school break to buy candy. *"Fissa, fissa"* when we were in Ifrane during the earthquake, a few years after the one that destroyed Agadir. The memory was still vivid. Morocco had buried its dead by the hundreds in quicklime in order to prevent an epidemic. The walls of our hotel room cracked, and crevices opened up in the courtyard. While I was buttoning my robe, Maco took my hand and begged me to leave. We had never heard a more terrifying sound than that of the angry earth and its echo in the mountains.

But we soon grew carefree again. Every night Maco and I, tucked into our twin beds, wondered if you could love a boy and still remain friends with him. If the heart was big enough for that.

Our mother spent a long time making herself up before going out. She was very beautiful and many men had fallen under her spell. That worried us. Didn't love require too many games and intrigues, too much coquettishness, and didn't that exclude true and sincere friendship? Could a woman in love remain a good friend?

Maco fell in love before I did. I felt that part of her no longer belonged to me and that made me sad. I came to the conclusion, wrongly, that a friend, in order to be reliable, should not be too much in love or too sensitive (which makes you touchy and complicated). I was afraid of the future. In those moments when Maco seemed far away, I would console myself with Young Werther.

You're not thick-skinned enough, my mother would say. But I had no desire to be. I would much rather have Young Werther as a friend than Captain Ahab.

Meanwhile Maco hid her packets of birth control pills in her teddy bear's ear and I covered for her. One night she escaped, climbing over the gate, and came back with marks on her neck. My father, furious, was waiting for her at the garden gate. He pulled off the Indian scarf that covered her neck. What is this? he asked, pointing to the red marks.

I remember Maco's little voice replying: "I'm allergic to carrots."

How did she come up with that?

We looked at each other. This was not the time to break into uncontrollable laughter, which in serious situations usually bent us double and brought tears to our eyes.

"Don't you remember, Papa?" I asked reproachfully. "Maco is very allergic to carrots."

And why was Corinne (he only called her Corinne when he was very angry) climbing over the garden gate?

My angelic sister replied, "To save a poor lost cat who was meowing in the night."

I rushed to help her: "Poor little cat, I would have been in tears."

My father, an authoritarian man, respected in his profession—he was a specialist in maritime law—gave in. With Maco and me, he always gave in.

Despite her adventures with boys, Maco reassured me that nothing had changed: "My heart is big enough. You'll see, yours will be too when you fall in love."

Me, fall in love? I loved only my horse and my wild boar. And books. My little sister would say, "When you read less, you'll start to live."

I read because I was afraid of life. I sought friendship because I was afraid of love.

I had been shocked by Dino Buzzati's hero, mistreated and humiliated by a young prostitute with whom he was madly in love, just as I had been irritated

by Madame Bovary's naïveté and annoyed by Anna Karenina's thoughtlessness.

Maco would not have repudiated Dino Buzzati's hero. He gambled. He lost. Too bad. It's not so far-fetched to say that love is like Russian roulette. Maco followed her heart, her only guide.

Our parents often argued in the hall. Sometimes right in front of our door. Even if we didn't want to hear, we understood the mutual recriminations. They didn't divorce, as I sometimes wished they would when they shouted too loudly late into the night.

At fifteen, friendship seemed more possible. One doesn't ask anything concrete of one's friend, and one spends more time thinking of him than living with him. What does friendship require but a bit of consideration, a bit of loyalty?

For Maco the magic of friendship was in sharing. It might begin with a cigarette (she already smoked at thirteen), continue with a piece of *zan* (licorice) floating at the bottom of her purse among the coins and shreds of tobacco, and move on to a shared secret.

She would share secrets to cement a friendship, but sparingly, never misjudging the person to whom she opened her heart. Maco, like the little dogs who always gravitate toward those who pet them, made no mistakes. She called that "having a nose," a sixth sense. She didn't need books. Books existed to console those who were melancholy and timid, life's unfortunates.

Mama worried. Not only because I buried myself in books. I think she considered my books rivals. They gave me answers that I think she would have liked to give me herself. For our ever-present mother, this was hard to bear. She told me that if I read too much, I would become nearsighted. She was right about that.

I attributed magical properties to books. They were like an abridged version of life, a digest of meaning that had to be constantly consulted in order not to lose one's way. We were so different, my sister and I. She used a different compass. Maco didn't need the consolation of books; she wanted to play. To be among the grown-ups, whom she observed with her child's gaze.

I wanted to write. I flitted over the pages, gathering nectar, seeking a sense of well-being, convinced that words would bring me a feeling of peace.

It was time for me to leave. My adolescence came to an end in the room we shared (since I never liked my own), with words and a giant poster of Elvis taped to our wall.

I *left behind* my horse, our room with its pink and gray curtains, and the twin bed next to Maco's, which was now empty. I left behind my friends from the beach and from school. I left behind my father and my mother, half-proud, half-worried to see me so determined. I left behind my diaries, after burning several of them. I left behind the sun, my carefree life, maybe because it was too easy. I left my first love, who was not a love at all because good sense had prevailed. I left the trees that I had planted and which must now be taller than I am.

I left Maco.

Maco was fourteen. She still sucked her thumb, sucking more greedily just before falling asleep. A filly with legs too long, somewhere between a rough-edged baby and a Mary Quant–style vamp. Torn between sadness that her big sister was leaving and happiness at having her room all to herself? Who knows.

In fact, the one I left behind was me. But I didn't mind leaving myself behind. The person I would have become if I had stayed didn't interest me.

I loved my childhood, but I was about to graduate. The only one with whom I could secretly prolong that childhood was Maco. "They say you'll be . . ."; "They say I'll be . . ."; or "When I grow up, I'll be . . ."—why shouldn't we dream, continue our litany of magic words and invented expressions, prolong happiness . . . be silly together?

When Maco came to Paris, she would bring with her the part of me that always remained with her and that came alive only when she was there. I wasn't going to leave her for long. Just three years. In three years she would graduate and come and join me. I would barely have time to get a place ready for her, to find her a studio apartment with a kitchenette and a cupboard full of dishes like the tea sets she had asked Santa Claus for not so long ago. I could find a university for her, help her choose her courses, introduce her to my new friends.

But one does not leave the country of one's childhood

without heartbreak or future consequences. Nothing in Paris resembled what I had known. My university friends had known one another since grade school and often their families had spent vacations together for years. I was the new girl wherever I went, dragging this difference around with me, without familiar reference points and at the same time not daring to admit to myself that I preferred my new world to the old one.

In spite of the age difference, my friends at home were Maco's friends. She saw them even when I was far away. She lived the life I could no longer lead, and that comforted me. But my real tie to her was the telephone, from which her voice bubbled miraculously. We would tell each other about our lives, so different and yet so alike in the way we experienced them. While she was prolonging the past, I prepared for the future. But aside from the distance, nothing had changed. Our concerns, our conversations remained the same.

Little by little, Maco and I got used to talking on the phone. We could tell each other so much even without seeing each other. She missed me, but less, it seemed, than I missed her. Even though she was my younger sister, I was the one who suffered and she was the one

who comforted me. That gave her a certain superiority, even though she hadn't sought it out.

I left in order to become strong, and I had never been so weak. I brought a photograph of Velvet Nose, the small bottle of orange blossom water Maco had slipped into my bag when I was leaving, and the words of my favorite authors, which I suspected my sister was happy to be rid of.

She spoke to me of sunshine, waterskiing on Bin-el-Ouidane Lake, flying down the snowy slopes of Oukaimeden. What could I offer her in return?

A tiny studio apartment that looked out over a sunless courtyard, freezing weather, a university of concrete and aluminum, sadness, evenings spent counting the days until the next vacation. Was it for her sake or mine that I asked her to join me? For mine, I'm sure.

If she had been with me, I would never have been depressed. If she had been with me, we would have laughed together, cackling like geese, hands clapped over our mouths if someone had caught us in the act. We would have plotted against all the guys in the world, would have learned how to be bitches and shrews, would have been the greatest, my little sister and me.

If she had been with me, I would never have done a bit of work, would have been out dancing in nightclubs every night, would have worn 501 jeans and long-sleeved Fruit of the Loom T-shirts with the sleeves rolled up, like her.

If she had been with me, I would have saved time and I wouldn't have become nearsighted.

When she got too excited about the life she was living, I worried. There were too many words like *cool*, *fab*, *awesome* in every sentence. It was clear to me that Maco would never have the willpower to give up the easy life she led. Besides, I had been wrong; I had underestimated the difficulties of leaving all on my own.

Every day I dreamed of the taste of bread cooked in an earthenware oven, the scent of fresh mint and co-riander in the kitchen garden. I could even feel once again the chill running up my spine when I ran home from school after a swim in the sea, a paper cone of fried squid in my hand, my long, dripping-wet braid slapping against my dark blue smock, beating out the rhythm of my steps, cooling me off.

I had brought my glove and black soap with me for nothing. No one here knew how to use them. Maco knew how to scrub the skin like a professional. She could have gotten a job in a hammam. But she was no longer with me. So every week I set out for the hammam in Paris, where I rediscovered the odors, the moisture, the heat of the baths of my childhood.

My shells were losing their sheen so far from the sea. And Liz and Claudia (Maco had entrusted them to me) had become strange and disturbing, like any dolls in an adult's house.

What I was most afraid of happened. Maco didn't show up for her exams. She chose to thumb her nose at social convention, preferring laughter, dancing, freedom.

She told me the news in her little voice, mind made up, pretending to be upset: I didn't study hard enough, she told me. And I didn't want to fail the exams. I think it was the opposite: she was afraid of succeeding. Who knows, the worst can always happen. Passing her exams would have meant coming to Paris and leaving behind her great love, whom she had already met.

I took it personally (why pass up another chance to suffer?) and was hurt. I certainly wasn't vigilant enough with Maco. I didn't know how to redirect her, cure her of her illusions, force her to act a certain way against her will. Friendships, even the strongest ones, run out of breath. One doesn't have the power to control the loved one's will, her life, her dark or weak or careless side.

Vain ambition. The only true friend lies within. If this friend deserts you, no one else can understand, can penetrate the outer shell, can help you. Not even the most loving mother, the most devoted sister.

Maco listened to the sirens' song. The man at her side undid everything I had worked so painstakingly to construct over the years.

I said: Paris. He said: Casablanca.

I said: studies. He said: absolutely not.

Understandable. He was in love.

Our father died before Maco was able to graduate. I think if he had lived he would have forced her to get her diploma. Maybe she wouldn't have married so young, and neither would I. We wouldn't have needed to look elsewhere for the protection and love we had lost.

Maco came to Paris after all. I was very surprised. So was she. Reluctantly she agreed to enroll at
the École du Louvre as an auditor. Nothing came of it.
She was in love. With whom? She wouldn't say. Then
the mystery man acquired a name, and the name a
known face.

I forgot about school for a few days and devoted
myself entirely to her. I became guide, chauffeur, sec-
retary. I went to great lengths to show her the more se-
ductive aspects of Paris. I took things slowly, as one
does with a fragile animal one wants to attract without
frightening it. But there wasn't much chance she
would catch the big-city bug. The Parisian scene didn't
interest her.

Other people, the world of appearances, all that
happened outside herself were like a light breeze that

could not touch her. She was not the type to want to shine and wondered why anyone would sacrifice the present for the future, living as one wanted for living for appearances, and especially, why one would trade love for studies and ambition.

She lived as a foreigner in Paris. Maco wriggled with impatience, a small meteor eager to return to her lover and the hot sun of her childhood. It was impossible for her to live life on a grand scale. She waited for life next to the telephone. Her heart leapt when it rang, and she was carried away when she spoke to him.

In the space of a fit of laughter, she became once again the mischievous little girl whose joy disappeared when she came up against etiquette, convention, conformity. I heard her laugh in a man's face when he asked for *cochonnaille*, pork sausages. She had never heard such a funny word. There was no stopping her. I had to give her a glass of Coca-Cola, pat her on the back, and take her outside to calm her down. For years afterward, all I had to do was say *cochonnaille* (with the Marseilles accent she adored) for her to burst out laughing all over again.

In the end the Louvre didn't want her. A few days after we mailed our request, we got the response: the enrollment lists were full.

I remember that letter, short and dry like a sentence with no possibility of appeal. Maco began to cry when she understood. An administrative stamp had dictated the decision she would never have dared to make so soon. She wanted to depend on a man, to be his captive, to be at his mercy.

Maco left Paris.

Maco got married.

She was happy to have her wings clipped by her fiancé. Maco didn't think like me anymore; she thought like him.

Deep down I understood her and admired her courage; she wanted to live her passion without limits. And because I understood her, I am angry at myself now for not being able to convince her to stay. My warnings rang false.

I couldn't stop Maco from leaving. I helped her close her suitcase and fill it with all the trinkets she had bought in fashionable boutiques. She was so happy at the idea of being with him again that she skipped in place or clapped her hands when speaking about him.

Maco was passionate. She was swept away by love, trusting, immoderate, like she was with life: incredibly spontaneous, entirely motivated by the dictates of her heart.

"You like it? Take it." Maco was always saying that. She said it just before telling me she was leaving when I complimented her on her T-shirt. Before I could even turn around, Maco was topless in our apartment, the T-shirt in her hand. "Take it. It's for you. And forgive me. . . ."

Forgive her? It was myself I couldn't forgive. I wasn't her big sister in this affair, I was her accomplice.

FLITTING ABOUT.

GATHERING HONEY.

Paris was too big for her. The Chinese proverb "Shrink your heart" and Cocteau's admonition "Do not step outside the chalk circle" fit her like a glove. One friendship too many and the circle overflows.

As beautiful as daylight, she captivated everyone she came in contact with; she believed that friendship was a business, a business of friendliness and congeniality. In Paris our "friends" had wings: they used them to flit about, gathering honey here and there, taking the best of everyone. So many flowers, so many different and interesting people to explore. Why limit yourself to two, three, five, or six flowers? Flowers scatter their petals to the wind. People are drawn to each other. Wasn't that enough?

People kissed each other hello, used *tu* with each other, invited each other until a minor misunderstanding toppled the beautiful edifice that had been constructed.

That frightened Maco. She did not venture into that world. She was happy with her own world, ruled by simple passions. She had her own friends. She had the sun to warm her. The beach to run on. The sky to escape to. She lacked nothing, not even love, which she was never without.

FAREWELL TO THE WORLD
OF CHILDHOOD

I *tried to convince* her not to get married. Not yet. I repeated over and over, "A woman should get a degree, have a profession."

But Maco, too much in love, didn't listen to me anymore. I hated to argue with her; she was so sensitive. If I hurt her feelings, she was capable of sulking for days on end and speaking to me so coldly that it drove me to despair.

I can still see her on that street in the Latin Quarter, running for a taxi to take her to Orly Airport so she could rejoin her beloved. In fact, it was the day that we parted. Maco left me standing there on the sidewalk, dumbfounded. I had not only lost my sister. My little sister had given me the one message I didn't want to accept: "We're grown-up now."

We would not see each other again for a long time. And it would never be the same again.

From that moment on our time together would be short and intense. Two or three days stolen here and there. Sleepless and exhausted, we would stay up all night talking so as not to lose any time, or to make it up.

THE THOUSAND AND ONE NIGHTS

On her wedding day, Maco spun around on the traditional large round tray, dressed as a Berber, covered in gold and emeralds, her face and hands tattooed with henna. A throng of women around her uttered strange sounds, tapping their mouths with their hands.

Maco dressed in a caftan embroidered with gold and emeralds, already pregnant; Maco in the kingdom of the Thousand and One Nights.

After that everything changed. Not our complicity, of course. Something else. Something in her eyes changed. Behind the euphoria, I sensed her uneasiness. She laughed as before, but her eyes didn't always follow. Soon I began to see signs of resignation in her.

Like in the photo that hung in my room. She is

leaning on her elbows in a cafe in Spain, her eyes too heavily made-up. Her sweater has slipped down, exposing a round burnished shoulder, tanned to a color between honey and cinnamon. But what one notices is the sadness in her black eyes.

When I look at my sister in this photo, I feel the transitory nature of things. Maybe she understood very early on how short life is and had the misfortune of knowing better than others that nothing really belongs to us. "I am beautiful and one day I will disappear. Look at me, immerse yourself in me if you love me" is the message she seems to be sending me, there, in the photo, in that café in Spain.

Maco was right to grow up faster than the others. In the kingdom of the Thousand and One Nights, the light went out of her eyes.

It's considered normal for an Arab wife to travel only with her family, to live at home, to avoid making friends at school. Until the day when nothing is normal anymore. When rebellion begins to brew, despite the birth of a second child.

I would have loved to be mistaken. But my premonitions tortured me, and I tried not to think about them, as though even my thoughts could harm her. When things became inescapable, I reassured her about her choice. We never again spoke of my reservations.

I got married just before she did. My way of responding, closing a door as well. Even though my marriage was less a betrayal of our childhood world than hers.

My husband was the same age as I was; he loved jokes and laughed with Maco. We met at university. We were kids. Maco married a man who was fourteen years older. She had to wear a caftan or a tailored suit with matching bags and shoes like her mother-in-law, run a household, entertain important people.

She left childhood behind before I did. To the point where I wondered where she had gotten the ideas for such refined meals, the bread plates she covered with little embroidered napkins. I would look at her, incredulous. And yet, when we saw each other again, she'd leave behind the perfect hostess, the Moroccan bourgeois housewife she had become, and revert to her former self.

I would ask Maco to imitate the James Browns of our nights in Casablanca when we danced to "Sex Machine," and she would gyrate, holding an imaginary microphone, moaning suggestively until we burst out laughing.

Do it again, Maco. Do the imitation of the Mohammeds (young Moroccan men who lived it up) *dancing to "Sex Machine."*

No one would have dared ask her to do any of this in front of her husband. Kidding around did not amuse the man in her life. It alarmed him.

But Maco didn't care. She had learned to belly dance for him, undulating to the music of Oum Kalsoum, arms circling, hands as light as birds fluttering above her head. For him she had learned to speak classical Arabic, the only written Arabic. For him she reserved another face, the face of love.

I too had been charmed by her Muslim husband, who was more intimidating in his current role than when I had first known him. I admired his daring when he became the first in his family to break with tradition, to oppose his father and marry a Catholic. But I knew that deep down he would never forgive her for it. Or rather that he would never forgive himself and she would have to pay for it. Intuition?

Kassim was elegant. Handsome. Refined. At his

house you didn't eat one or two courses, but ten, served on low tables, and you didn't sit on chairs, you reclined on cushions. Maco loved him. He wore white robes and yellow leather slippers that made him look like an Arabian prince.

Can you stop someone from loving another on the basis of intuition?

My intuition was logical. I knew Maco better than anyone else in the world. I knew that she rose every morning to look at the sun. I knew she couldn't stand bras, closed shutters, constraints of any kind.

I knew she was a whirlwind, a little bird who burst out laughing at nothing, who flirted when she was twelve, smoked at thirteen, ran away at fourteen. And I knew that no one would ever tame her.

I also knew how wealthy Moroccan families lived. Maco, madly in love, left behind her motorbike and the Lyautey lycée in order to receive government ministers in villas covered with Persian carpets.

For a while.

In *the early months* of her pregnancy, she would twirl around in front of him so that he could admire her figure before the child ruined it. She grew sad when he resumed his freedom as a Muslim man. Nothing serious, as far as he was concerned. But Maco didn't see it like that. In spite of her sisters-in-law's and her mother-in-law's fatalism, Maco, raised in different circumstances, could not bear infidelity.

She converted to Islam; Corinne became Leila. She tattooed her hands and feet with henna, invited guests for the *ftour*, the evening meal during Ramadan. But she loved according to the dictates of her heart. Beyond custom, beyond religion. Love cannot be shared. And no sage, no woman from his family could convince her otherwise.

When the first signs of betrayal—letters, perfume,

feminine lingerie—confirmed her suspicions, Maco, already resigned, called in the *adul* (notary in charge of marriages and divorces) and asked for a divorce.

Just as love does not necessarily come into being with the signing of a piece of paper in the presence of the mayor, so it does not always die with a divorce. The rest of the story was long, complicated, and painful.

Maco, exhausted but free, far removed from the problems that arose one after the other, returned to our parents' house. The children went back and forth between the two houses. Kassim, convinced that she would come back, that divorce was merely a way to get her back more submissive than before, waited. He had not yet laid down the law that would govern their relationship and which Maco could never have imagined.

In Morocco, the man has all the power.

For a few weeks Maco took refuge in our mother's arms, in her old pink and gray room, which she had kept unchanged, from the Elvis poster to the written quotes we had left behind. Stuffed with the yogurt cake and meatballs with tomato sauce and coriander that she loved, she enjoyed a brief carefree period. Freed from all constraints, she took advantage of simple pleasures, traded in her suits for her favorite taboo 501 jeans with the holes in the knees, threw away her quilted purse and took up her straw basket once again. The old records were unearthed; her friends came back. She found her closets as she had left them, stuffed with out-of-fashion dresses from her adolescence.

Because she was heedless and unhappy, Maco freed herself from her chains. She wanted another, simpler life; she wanted another man, one who liked to sleep on the beach, surf, drive a go-cart, use a computer, whip up a sauce in the kitchen, end up at La Notte or the Tube in the middle of dozens of young Moroccans imitating James Brown, a man her own age, faithful, with a heart as big as the house she had fled from. A man who was hers alone. Was Maco's heart big enough, at least for a while, to love two men? Did she love them both?

Did the man who had the courage to defy his family for love of her punish her in Islamic fashion in order to return to the tradition he could not forgive himself for having rejected? Or did he punish her because Maco had sought consolation in the arms of another man?

Who was this other man, who loved her to the point of accepting her, wounded as she was, haunted by her former husband, crying for her children all day long? He was her savior, her guardian angel, the one who enabled her to bear what was unbearable.

Maco left her husband's house with no rights and without a cent, but she didn't care. She left behind the luxury she was accustomed to without regret. The new man in her life welcomed her, took care of her, struggled with her, and loved her children as if they were his own.

After nine years of loving him, when at last she allowed herself to give a child to the man who wanted one so much, she flew away, forever.

Hello, Chris, it's Maco.

Hello, Maco, it's Chris.

That's how our conversations began, depending on who called the other.

How could I ever have stood our separation if it weren't for this machine that brought me Maco's voice? Of course we wrote to each other. But letters took too long to arrive and Maco's problems were always urgent.

"Chris, I need to speak to you. . . ."

And Maco would recount the latest installment in the serialized novel of her life.

It was always passionate, always exciting, whether she was in paradise or suffering the tortures of hell. Maco had staked everything on love. And love took up so much space in her, created such suffering that it ruled her existence. She risked a lot choosing a man whose background was so different from hers. She risked her life. But then, she liked living on the razor's edge.

Stubborn idealist that she was, she threatened separation and divorce at the first misstep while her husband looked on, amused, unable to believe that a Muslim woman (for that is what she had become), the mother of two children, would actually go through with it. Maco rejected him with the same intensity with which she had once desired him and set her mind on getting him.

I shared each installment, each allusion, each reconciliation and flight that made up their love story. I shared it all, thanks to the telephone, which made me feel even more powerless and frustrated to be so far away from her.

Would Maco and I have been so close if we hadn't been so far away from each other? Would we have made the same imaginative effort to understand each other's universe if we had lived in the same city?

There would not have been the same festive feeling every time we met. Our meetings would never have been banal, but we would have taken them for granted, it would have been normal. And Maco and I, at heart, hated normalcy.

Maco gave me everything she had left to give.

"And you, Chris, tell me . . ." she would say as soon as she had recovered a bit of inner peace.

My problem was more hidden. I was ashamed to be depressed, to be heartsick, ashamed of the indefinable pain that arose out of nowhere and that I couldn't understand. I knew that it lurked inside me and provoked me to detach myself rather than fight. I was running away from myself. There were reasons for it, of course, but unlike Maco's situation, no one was hurting me.

Maco had never been depressed. She made fun of me and my "shrink." How can a guy seated behind you, who never speaks, cure you? Maco had her own technique when she was down. Introspection was not her forte; she was more likely to open a good bottle of Bordeaux and bulldoze over her worries.

Maco's problems were too rooted in reality for her to fight against them with the weapons of this world. She fought pain with pleasure, sadness with joy, worry with the proper medicine. She could face, confront, find a response.

Except for the loss of her children. For that she had

no solution. It was an open wound that no one and nothing, except the children's presence, could salve.

Maco knew everything about my life. I didn't even know whether she had held my new baby in her arms, or slept in my new apartment, or if I had simply described them to her. All the phantom places, the faraway shadows, she spoke so convincingly of them that she planted the seed of doubt in my mind. What was the truth?

Maco lived my life as I lived hers. Maybe she thought she didn't need to study because I was doing it, and maybe I thought I could leave our childhood because she stayed.

I'm *angry with God*. I have my reasons, like everybody else. Each one of us maintains an indefinable relationship with Him, a one-sided dialogue. The mind focuses, but never reaches a conclusion. None of this concerns me. My mother-in-law used to say to me, "If God ever existed, He died in Auschwitz."

If He ever existed, He died of sorrow long before that, I'm afraid.

I envy those with whom God stops to have a drink. He has never come to my house. Maco, on the other hand, wore the cross from her baptism as well as a miniature Koran from her first marriage around her neck and invoked several gods when Kassim so harshly laid down the law and life became too hard: Maco could only see her six-year-old daughter and nine-month-old son once a week. No weekends. No vacations together.

The carefree days were at an end, the days of sudden laughter and fooling around. The time of tears began. Maco suffered her punishment, which never let up.

From that moment on, it was always me who came to see her and my niece and nephew. The first time, I arrived on a Saturday morning. Maco never had her children on Saturday. I thought because I had come so far and wasn't always there that I would be allowed to see them. But at that time there were no exceptions to the rules imposed by her ex-husband.

Maco's fear annoyed me. Even when it was just the two of us, she didn't dare to rebel. She was afraid of my reaction and wouldn't allow me to help her. Maco double-locked her doors when she wanted to talk, suspicious of those around her. She felt the walls had ears.

She did not want to risk losing the few hours a week she had. I pleaded with Maco to listen to me, to consult a lawyer in France, to let me speak to Kassim. She wept and begged me not to do anything, afraid he would take revenge. As though there could be anything worse than allowing a mother to see her children only once a week.

But she broke the rules. Later, when her children were old enough to go to school, she went there every morning. Hidden in her car, she watched them arrive, not wanting to miss a single chance to see them. The chauffeur, who had seen her, took pity on her. He allowed her to rebraid her daughter's hair ("Papa isn't very good at braiding," said the girl), to smooth their collars, and to hug them in the street.

I came back one Wednesday and saw the children at Maco's, huddled in her arms. They looked like two puppies curled up against their mother's stomach. Then they left, dragged off by the chauffeur, clutching the nightgown she had worn the night before, in order to have her scent with them.

She never cried in front of the children. Only when she was alone, shut up in her room. In front of them, she defended their father, the importance of learning the Koran and classical Arabic, and the importance of a strict upbringing. She encouraged them to respect their family and their culture. The most important thing was the children's happiness. But when they asked her, "Why can't we stay longer with you?" she didn't know how to answer.

Maco had dark circles under her eyes. The presents

I brought her from Paris no longer amused her. Not even my presence. Nothing was important to her anymore except seeing her children and knowing whether, after eight years of this arrangement, she could take them skiing. "Do you think he'll let me?" I can still hear her asking me. "Three days. Just three days."

After her divorce, Maco lived only to know the answer to these questions. How many times did I mourn along with her over this?

Wherever I went, I invited her to join me. After her divorce, she came to Corsica for twenty-four hours, and as Marrakech wasn't too far from Casablanca, she came for half a day. Maco was traumatized. She no longer wanted to leave home, to travel. She didn't want anything that seemed like a separation. She did not want to leave the land of her children; even if she couldn't see them, she knew they were nearby, they breathed the same air she did, they saw the same evening star before going to bed.

So during many painful years, I came to her because she could no longer go anywhere. For a long time it had been impossible to talk to Maco without her crying, since her heart had been broken, her insides torn out, her children taken away from her. Because she missed them and suffered migraines from the anguish that burned in her chest, veins, and throat, Maco could no longer speak of anything else. She was suffering too much.

I have always been convinced that her ex-husband acted this way because he loved her, to maintain his power over her and force her to come back. Simplistic, maybe. But I was not mistaken. Not long before, Maco told me with tears in her eyes, he had come to ask her to marry him again.

Maco was overwhelmed. Kassim had been her first love. She wasn't even sixteen when they met. He had made her suffer so much she couldn't imagine he could love her. The declaration of love came too late. Maco didn't budge. But Kassim had won. Anguish and guilt had destroyed her happiness with the man who had, over the past years, kept her head above water. Maco loved him. Her relationship with Kassim was shattered forever. Too many tears had been shed. She could not have her children see her as a victim. With this adult no, Kassim understood that Maco would never come back and he modified the rules, up to a certain point.

The children could see their mother more often but could never leave the country with her, not even for vacations. For many years, the children were the victims of a lover's blackmail.

For her last Christmas, Maco was hoping to bring them to her house in Spain, to the house she loved and which they had never seen even though Cabo Negro, the tip of North Africa overlooking the Mediterranean where the children spent their vacations, wasn't far away. Just across the water, a boat ride away. But Maco's children were known at every border crossing. She discovered this quite by accident, when a girl with the same name as her daughter was stopped and prevented from crossing the border.

And yet, if the children managed to survive the painful separation from their mother, it was thanks to their father. A strange father, monster and teddy bear in quick succession. Thanks to a father who loved them to the point of taking on the role of the mother from whom he had taken them. Kassim dressed them, brushed their hair, and took them into bed with him at night.

I was overwhelmed by Maco's sadness. We still laughed, but only about the past. The pain of the present went too deep to allow us the slightest lightheart-edness.

"Do you think he'll let me take the children to the mountains? Three days. Just three days . . ." Always the same refrain. How I would have loved to be able to promise her this.

One *day my shrink* said to me, "The heart is not a cake to be divided up into slices. The heart is inexhaustibly rich; you can love many people in a lifetime, alternately, one after the other, or at the same time."

I don't like this theory; I want to believe that we are made for only one great love and three or four friends in this lifetime. Five people in all who are there for us, whom we can find when we need them. Not a hundred. I didn't know that I would find only one unconditional friend, my sister, Maco. I didn't have to look far for her. She slept in a twin bed next to me. She crumpled the wrappers of the candy she crunched loudly at night, and always opened the shutters in our room too early so she could see the sun rise. "Chris, come here, look. . . ." I would get out of bed, kneel next to her and we would watch the spectacle.

Maco, in spite of her suffering, was always giving, through her words and her warmth. Even when she was wounded. She was my comprehensive insurance policy. I could wander far from home, deep into the jungle, and approach wild animals, and know that when I got home, I could pick up the phone and hear her calm and reassuring voice, so understanding of my problems and weaknesses.

Every time I strayed into situations that were too complicated, where I asked for more than the other could give, when I was annoyed by the limitations of some and the stupidity of others, she forgot her own problems for a moment and unraveled the knots for me with her words, her humor and understanding. "Chris," she would say, "what have you gotten yourself into this time?" She would scold me: "You can't change people. Not even yourself." And I would feel like a small adventurous cat, exploring regions too vast for her.

Unfortunately, Maco never got used to my life or the people in it. Maco loved the Ain Diab beach, her Range Rover, the game of belote, afternoons, Johnny and Billie Paul. She loved to cook, to dance, to be surrounded by children. And she loved sunrises. In her own mind, Maco never really left our cabin at the end of the garden: she remained faithful.

We lived on two different planets and yet I don't think two beings could have been closer, more complicitous, than we were. Maybe in spite of everything I was a bit like her and she was a bit like me. Blood ties? I find that theory unsatisfactory. I don't like the idea of shared blood, shared genes; it makes me feel sick.

I think I loved her for who she was, not because she was my little sister.

One night my little sister died.

One night the person I thought was indestructible went away and abandoned me.

One night the one who brought me so much joy and happiness hurt me very deeply.

One night Maco left this world and her earthly shell.

She could no longer see; her eyes were sealed shut for eternity and her body was cold. Icy to the touch. Maco no longer looked like herself.

All of a sudden the little bird who loved to sing fell from her nest. The pain in my heart was so great, as though I had been stabbed with a knife, that I can't write these words without feeling it still and weeping.

The other's death begins with pain, a physical pain, followed by emptiness, a void, a terrible suffering that, they say, later strengthens you. As though the other's strength enters into you and inhabits you. You become two and are never alone.

I'm no longer there. I sigh all day long, breathing in cruelty, breathing out pain. But the pain doesn't go away.

Now that Maco is no longer here, I have to continue this interrupted dialogue on my own, respond for her, go on alone. From now on everything will depend on my inner strength or weakness. The strength of my actions and my thoughts, all will depend on me alone. I feel old before my time.

Maco's short life has been added to mine. We have become a pair of phantom tightrope walkers. I walk with her on my shoulders. I sway. It's hard to take on thirty-five years all of a sudden, hard to manage both of us inside my head. I have to get rid of the superfluous and hold on to the essential, keeping her intact.

Now whenever I come face-to-face with a situation, I have two responses. Hers and mine. All is well as long as we agree, but what about when we don't? I would rather let Maco's response win out, let her make use of my body, which she inhabits, so she can bring it back to life. I'm the one who is dead without her. Can one bring back the dead by voicing their ideas, lending them our bodies?

How will I survive her?

We never discussed this. I ask her advice but she doesn't answer.

Only religion provides an answer. When I was given a holy medal on the day of her funeral, I was told maybe it was better like this: she was going to a better world, eternity, the great beyond. Wherever she is, Maco is happy. The songs, the incense that stings your throat, the organ, the flowers, the congregation, the prayers: that is how we attempt to celebrate the mystery.

Religion must have been invented by the first orphans. But I refuse to be consoled. Even if it's unbearable, one must accept the unacceptable. My little sister is dead. She died without knowing whether she could at last take her children to the mountains for three days. She died after I told her I planned to write a book on friendship. Neither of us knew then that she would be the heroine of this book. Would she have been if she hadn't gone away? I'm sure she would have. All my thoughts about friendship lead to Maco.

I was so lucky to have known her from the time she

was born, to have grown up with her, to have seen the one who had always been my friend grow up. But there was the terrible distance. Maco had become a voice that sang "Happy Birthday" to me every October third in our special language, incomprehensible except to us.

This language died with her. I am now its sole custodian.

Whom can I talk to about things that would overwhelm even the dearest friends? The dark nights of the soul, the dark sides of the moon. No one but her, who so quickly turned into the "big sister," a role we exchanged, depending on the circumstances.

"Every man is alone and no one cares about anyone else and our sorrows are a desert island." So begins *The Book of My Mother* by Albert Cohen.

That's where I am: grieving, on a desert island.

All day long I think of her young body enclosed in a white tomb, far away, in Ben m'sik, a cemetery swept by the sea breeze and the prayers from the mosque. I think of her second burial, the final one, in a cave, which I couldn't go to because I had to keep our mother away and lie to her in order to protect her.

I think of Maco, who is here, now, as well as over there; she is everywhere and nowhere, she no longer answers the phone in her hoarse drawl, she no longer answers my letters. In our secret language I ask her if she thinks it's nice to abandon me like that, to leave me alone on this earth, alone in my house, with all the crafty people there are in the world.

When people compliment me on my dress, I hear myself say, "It's a silk caftan my sister brought back from Mecca." Mecca, the Orient, the colors, the words, joyous as at a celebration. No one can imagine the sadness they evoke in me. I inherited this caftan from my little sister, who is dead, and I can open all her drawers, help myself to everything of hers, her toys, her makeup, her music. . . . Even if I emptied her closet she wouldn't say anything. She can't defend herself against my pranks or against anyone at all. People can hurt her; she can no longer respond.

That's not true.

No one can hurt Maco anymore. And that's why I weep, because she is beyond the reach of pain.

Someone told me the story of an old man who became a widower after sixty years of marriage and, facing his wife's empty armchair, read the condolence letters he had received.

Maco was thirty-five years old. Thirty-five years of

friendship. I am a bit like the old widower. And yet I'm ashamed of how happy I feel when I find a good picture of Maco, or when a sip of hot tea warms my numb, motionless body.

The moments of respite don't last long. I never really forget the sorrow that hangs over me.

I wrote down the name of the White City, as they call it over there, where Maco is buried in the earth along with our childhood. Now I alone remember our huts under the table and in the closet; Liz and Claudia, our Barbie dolls who invited each other for dinner; Elvis Presley, whom Maco married at the end of the garden, holding a record cover. As for me, I was in love with Napoleon. Waiting for him to return, I organized her "weddings," a school, a theater so she and her classmates could perform. Elvis and Bonaparte brothers-in-law? Why not!

THE SONG OF THE MAUSOLEUM AND THE PRIEST'S PRAYER

Maco died on the eve of Ramadan. When they buried her, there was the sound of thunder and lightning, and the song of the mausoleum rose up to the heavens along with the priest's prayer. A good omen, said my former Muslim brother-in-law. Maco's true religion was love. She believed only in her two husbands. Hand in hand, bent by grief, they reconciled over her grave after having hated each other for so many years. I heard the Muslim say to the priest, "She gave so much and received so little." He knew what he was talking about. He was the one who had refused to give her her children when she pleaded with him and who would not grant her the three days for a ski trip that she was still hoping for the day before she died. But this time, Kassim was simply late in giving her his answer. Maco, do you hear? He told me that and he seemed sincere. He was crying. You can take the children with you. But it's too late, Kassim, too late.

So many tears shed for ten years, so much bad blood (an apt expression) to finally end up here. Poor little sister. Her love of life evaporated with the loss of her children. Maco was almost always sad and she no longer burst into laughter when, against her will, I dragged her to those evenings where she imagined that the chandelier in the living room would fall on the professor's illustrious head and she would shriek with laughter at the idea of it, surrounded by these sophisticated people who bored her so much.

I will always remember the pain that coursed through me when I was told of my sister's death, my racing heart, my wild eyes, as though I were trying to bring her back to life.

"My sister is dead." I cannot absorb it. It eludes me, I can't grasp it, I can't believe it.

My sister had been dead for six hours and no one dared to tell me. Neither of her husbands, nor my mother. It was midnight. Mama wanted to wait until the next day so I could have one last good night in my

life. Mama, in despair at having lost one daughter, worried that the remaining daughter would be in such pain it would kill her too.

One night when my husband and I got home from a dinner party, the baby-sitter told me to call my sister's house immediately—it was an emergency. I knew right away that something terrible had happened. Maco went to bed early so she could get up at dawn to go and brush her children's hair before they left for school and murmur words of love in their ears.

No sooner had I dialed Maco's number than an unknown voice answered. I heard a commotion when I said it was me. No one wanted to speak to me. There was a lot of noise on the other end and I called out to Maco. "Maco? Maco? What's happening?" Then I asked for her husband, the current one. He refused to come to the phone. The noise continued. Then a long silence. I hung up and called back. The second time Maco's friend Annie gave me the terrible news in mournful tones.

With Maco, I was still a child; I no longer am. Do you remember when we went to school together for the first time? I silently ask. You wore a sky blue and white apron with little donkeys embroidered on the pockets. What an idea! Your eyelids were still puffy from sleep, which made you look Chinese. Hanging on to Mama's skirts, we were terrified when they suddenly pushed us into the school yard.

Maco soon became more resourceful than me. In spite of the four-year difference in age, she smoked and flirted before I did, and early on she liked doing both, whereas tobacco made me cough and I preferred my horse to boys.

I'm so unhappy, I say. I call you and you don't answer. You're asleep forever. Is it possible?

Maco always answered me: from her bath, from the kitchen, even from her sleep. "Did I wake you?" "No, it doesn't matter." Does it still not matter? Now that everything is over and she is silent forever, I have to believe this reality that goes against the natural order of things. Maco was a daughter, a wife, a young mother, a future mother, a little sister; she wasn't supposed to die. Can one moment destroy thirty-five years of friendship? It's absurd.

I'm speaking to you. Are you asleep? Are you looking at me? Does it hurt? What's it like where you are? Or don't you know?

The indifference of the dead.

The last time we spoke, when Maco told me she was expecting a baby, I felt there was something making her unhappy. How could she tell Kassim the news? She was afraid he would react with fury and make his rules harsher and that would be the end of any hope of taking her children to the mountains. We were going to talk about it at greater length and try to figure out the best way not to send him into a rage. We didn't have time. A few hours later she went away forever; she expired along with all the worries she had lived with.

I should have called her back, but something came up that afternoon and I couldn't. An unimportant matter deprived me of the last moment of happiness I would feel when, curled up on a comfortable sofa, I allowed myself to be alone with her, and we told each other about our lives, and helped each other.

Can't God understand that He made a mistake? One does not reclaim a woman who is about to give birth. One does not take away a mother adored by her two children, who have already suffered too much by being separated from her. Doesn't God ever give back what He has taken away?

Poor children, hand in hand, kneeling next to their mother's coffin, mouths pressed against the wooden partition, as though seeking her warmth one last time.

I hug the children as I hugged their mother for the last time at Nouasseur Airport. They have the same shoulders as she, so frail when shaken by sobs.

I have the impression it's she I'm embracing. She who is crying because I'm about to leave. But there is a coffin in front of us. Which makes any hope of escape impossible. We are three orphans whom she is no longer able to love. Three abandoned orphans who have no idea what happens to the dead. She is dead. The way she would laugh at a silly word, her mischievousness, the way she danced to "Sex Machine," her excitement when she was about to go fishing. Everything is dead. Pain too. Everything has disappeared, as though nothing has ever existed. Nothing matters; so much the better if she never graduated, if she smoked, ran away, followed her own stubborn ideas.

So long live her carrot allergy, the kitty meowing in the night; long live Oukaimeden, Bin-el-Ouidane Lake; long live Elvis, Billie Paul, Johnny, James Brown, Lycra, low-cut bras, 501 jeans, and all the clothes from the Latin Quarter and Jamaa el Fna

Square; long live the men who loved her. Down with the Louvre, Young Werther, snobs, the Goody Two-shoes and bores of the world.

I see unhappiness everywhere I look.

Mama, leaning on the arm of her son-in-law, who, after his last night with his wife and baby, is incapable of consoling anyone. Poor man. He wanted to give them a house with a garden and ended up giving them a mausoleum in the cemetery. My only consolation is that she did not witness the spectacle surrounding her death.

Great unhappiness serves no purpose. I didn't need it to know that I loved her and that I couldn't live without her. Unhappiness has taught me nothing.

Only the awareness of that fraction of a second, cosmically speaking, that separates the moment of my death from hers gives me any relief. My sister will have preceded me by very little. I will soon be like her, lying under the earth, weighed down by rain and silence, motionless, floating in a dress that is now too big, stretched out all alone, like her, pitifully abandoned, with two children and a husband to weep for me.

How to say: "My sister died yesterday"? I heard myself utter these words in a disembodied voice as though someone else were speaking. Not me. Not my sister. Someone else. Yet I have to repeat to myself the terrible truth in order to take it in. "My sister is dead." The brain cannot register these words, not all at once, not right away. I could go on not speaking of it in order not to believe it, to push away the terrible news, until the inescapable hits home. Her pale beauty frozen for eternity, she will no longer feel cold, heat, hunger . . . nothing.

The happiness of believing my sister still alive would only be a trick, a stay of execution, and the immense unhappiness lurking behind that deception would lie in wait for me like a wild animal ready to pounce, eager for her blood, her flesh, her youth, waiting for a moment of distraction in order to devour her.

My sister is dead because I did not go and take her to the hospital, even if she didn't want to go. Dead because I didn't know that a low platelet count could mask a serious illness. Dead because I did not prevent her from conceiving this child. Dead because I was not at her side when, like a candle flame in a gust of wind, she weakened and died. Dead because I lived far away from her.

It was Annie, her best friend, who told me. No one

else had the courage. Is that too one of the responsibilities of a friend?

Before I got there, she had dressed my sister. She chose an ugly light blue jacket that I didn't want anymore and that Mama had taken out of my closet in Paris. Why in the world dress her in that hideous jacket? Then she put her in a bathrobe and a heavy pair of socks as though she could still catch cold. Maco, who loved only black, leotards, Lycra, low-cut bras—when she wore a bra—and wasp waists.

I was on the plane. Red eyelids, my nose buried in Kleenex. I was on the saddest trip imaginable to the land of my childhood. Probably for the last time. I will never return to the Ben m'sik cemetery.

I made up her face. No one had thought to touch up her lifeless skin, to apply bronze blush, to powder her cheeks with the big brush from her dressing table, slow upward strokes to bring out her cheekbones, caressing her one last time.

No one had thought to place next to her heart some photos of the children she had loved so much, too much, if one can love too much, or the white plush duckling, its beak against her cheek to kiss her when no one else could anymore.

I was afraid to look at her. I had to, though—it was the last time.

I was afraid to look at this last image.

I would have liked to remember only the next-to-last image of her.

When she went with me to the Nouasseur Airport in Casablanca, she treated me like a child she was responsible for. She called a porter, ran to buy me magazines she didn't know I had read two weeks before, some chewing gum so my ears wouldn't hurt when the plane took off and landed, a bottle of Moroccan rosewater because she knew I adored that perfume.

We cried as we kissed good-bye. She said, "Aren't we silly, Chris, to cry like this . . ." Not so silly. I felt her frail shoulders in my hands. "I'll stay until the plane takes off."

I watched her the whole time as I walked; she stood on tiptoe, waving her small hand behind the glass, then I couldn't see her anymore—she was lost in the crowd.

I want to hold on to this image. I want to forget the lifeless form in the room where the walls are covered with her children's collages, cut out with love, with those objects she wove out of cloth, the cupboards filled with her bathing suits and underwear, a vase of cut roses above her head, which, like her, would soon die.

And yet I know that this image, unacceptable, unimaginable, will haunt me and superimpose itself on all my other memories of her forever.

Do books have a destiny? I would say more likely a path. They lead us where we didn't know we were going.

You left at the beginning of this book, which has led me back to you.

I must continue the friendship alone, with only images and memories for support. I have no film of you, no tape recording. I couldn't bear to look at you or hear you. To hear your voice captured on a machine, imprisoned on earth after you yourself have left.

Now you only speak inside the heads of those who love you, those who go in search of you and beg for a sign. A sign you could give to those who wait for you, a sign invented by the imaginations of the unhappy people who cannot live without you.

Just yesterday, at the flea market in Paris—I know,

you used to make fun of that jumble, that chaos of countless objects displayed on the sidewalk—you kept speaking to me in our childhood language with its strange intonations, to tell me it was awful and that I was a bit eccentric to like such a horrible place. At the flea market, jostled by the crowd, I cried and you made me laugh. Yes, I laughed the way I used to, right there, in front of the rusty iron, the cracked glass, the kitschy Vallauris and Clichy vases.

"My sister is crazy. . . ." I can hear you. You had had enough. You wanted to go back to Saint-Germain and spend some time looking in the clothing boutiques you liked or go back to Morocco, to your house, so we could sit in front of the low table and eat crepes: *barjhrie, lemsemen, rjhaif*—words that are unpronounceable in French, that you knew in Arabic, and that were the dishes set before me whenever I came to visit.

Is it in these moments when you are so present that you are alive in me? Or are you dead, in the cemetery of the White City, and is it me, poor me, who is still alive despite your absence, who continues to conjure you up because I can't go on without you?

Life doesn't interest me if we can't discuss it together.

I still hear you saying, "You mustn't ever again be depressed now that you have two children." You said it to me another time when I came back from a fitness club I wanted to take you to. "It's good to belong to a fitness club," you said. "It gives you a tight bottom." But I ride the stationary bike in order to be more relaxed when I write. I concentrate better when I've exercised a bit. Colette, according to her housekeeper, preferred to work on a full stomach, face to the wall. As for me, I need infinity before me, with my body feeling light and relaxed.

Colette doesn't interest you. I know. Sorry. You told me that my books were the only ones you liked to read.

I am writing this book so I can talk to you and talk about you. So I can describe your beautiful face, your heavily mascaraed eyelashes, which I see fluttering before me, your slender body that a gust of wind could knock down, your laughter, which echoes in my ears.

You don't ask for anything. Did you ever ask me for anything in your short life? Nothing. You gave. As for posterity, the opinion of others, recognition, none of this meant anything to you, not even envy. You only wanted a place in our hearts, that's all you wanted.

You wouldn't have wanted me to talk about you in a book, even a small one. Forgive me, you who loved to live hidden, for evoking your passion for paper collages, your unique way of cutting out the world and pasting it back together according to your own vision, for exposing your gift for color and harmony, your coded, surrealist-style messages à la Jacques Prévert or Max Ernst. You would have found it vulgar and inappropriate for me to brag about these things.

But let me do it out of sorrow, let me console myself as best I can, let me give to you imagining that you can still receive, let me steer the boat, now that you have disembarked.

Yesterday I phoned you. Stupidly. To make sure that your husband hadn't missed the plane. I listened to the phone ringing for a long time. I waited. There was no longer anything to wait for. You would never again answer.

When you were unsure, did you call me? I was far away; I couldn't help you. You called Mama, your husband, you hurriedly had your children taken away and announced to your housekeeper, who was next to you, that the end was near. I am haunted by this moment. When you knew. When you felt it.

A sudden flash in your head and, telephone in hand, you collapsed. Painlessly.

The last conversation I had with you was a very happy one. Far removed from the misery and death that awaited us. I can still hear your laughter, the joy of a pregnant woman whom, alas, no doctor had advised against a third pregnancy, despite your circulation problems. Your carefree attitude fooled me.

I didn't suspect anything. She is finally happy, I thought. It would be difficult to tell her not to keep the baby, to talk to her about sonograms and spinal taps rather than baby clothes. She wanted so much to be happy.

But the doctors saw it coming, they knew. How did you fool them, move them to the point of silencing them? Your general practitioner told me, weeping, "I couldn't stop her . . . she wanted so much to have this child. . . ."

Murderer. Why didn't he call me? I would have talked to you. I didn't know. You didn't want to worry me, you thought you could overcome your health problems by ignoring them. You used to say, It works or it doesn't. A small vein burst in that head I thought was so hard.

I toyed with the idea of being an aunt again for only a single day. You didn't prepare me for this tragedy, you gave me no warning at all. Nothing.

Maybe I didn't rebel enough at your death. I accepted it, I took in your friend Annie's words without challenging them. I believed her. The first lie, the coma, I swallowed it all. As I fainted, lying flat on the floor, overcome with sorrow, I gave in to fate. Gave in, bent, flattened, powerless.

I didn't fight against it. Maybe through sad experience. At twenty I fought against my father's death. I tried to resist, to deny, not to believe the doctor, to impose my own law, the law of my desires. A trial of strength that was useless for fighting against bitter fate. I left this world. In my head, I left. Because I couldn't see him anymore, my spirit followed him. I lost, thinking I had won. He did not come back and I had the impression of wandering through life like a wooden puppet, deprived of my senses. Never again. I'd rather die. I remember the line by Mallarmé, which at that time never left my mind: "You who know more of nothingness than the dead." The fate of the living dead. The living who are dead or the dead who are still living.

As hellish as hell itself.

ONE DAY I WON'T

HAVE TO DIE AS MUCH

Death always wins in the end. Now there's nothing left to do but weep.

I didn't weep for my father. I followed him. Now I weep for my sister.

The living dead don't weep, but the living do.

Do tears ease the pain? Isn't it shameful to try and feel better? Shameful to cry in order to ease the sadness?

I weep and sometimes I'm ashamed of how much better I feel than when I'm weighed down by sadness. I weep, therefore I am alive. To hold back the tears, to drown inside like before, what good does it do?

Is one stronger if one doesn't love? If one has no friends, no love, no Maco? Because human beings are so fragile that they can exist one day and disappear the next, to love is to take the risk of dying as many times as one loves. One goes on, shattered, until, on the day of one's own death, there is nothing left to die.

With Maco gone, there will be less in me to die, less to leave behind. My childhood has already disappeared and now, with her, all the laughter, the complicity, the secrets, the special moments. For this, I'm already dead. For this, I mourn endlessly. Certain subjects I could share only with her I keep quiet about, keep quiet about our secrets. Serious subjects, funny subjects, buried forever. There are areas of silence in my head. Areas of darkness. The lights have gone out. It's night and she will never return.

She is dead. That's how it is. She, with her stubborn little head, who did not want to take care of herself. Who did not want to travel without her husband. Who laughed at my anxieties. She died of stubbornness. Died because she hoped to spend a few days with her children. Died because she wanted to conceal her pain so that we wouldn't worry.

Maco, whom I love and who never could see farther than the tip of her own nose. She was incapable of calculation, of laying plans, of self-interest. Maco, who never aged, who was buried still perfect beneath the earth, which should receive only those who, late in life, have exhausted life's joys and pains. Maco, who defied logic and justice. Maco, who left just as she was about to give birth.

Is it possible that the embryo of a two-month-old baby could have survived after she died? And that no one came to the aid of this beginning life that would slowly be snuffed out by suffocation, thirst, hunger, cold, who knows? How long did the little creature outlive its mother?

Maco wanted a little girl. Her name would have been Marie.

Dead?

Died laughing, died of fright.

Maco supplied the coordinates of my past. The more one moves forward, the more one needs to know who one is.

In my disjointed life—two countries, two husbands, three very different social groups—Maco remained constant. Sister, friend, the one who knew everything, understood everything, my parallel destiny. Now I am cast adrift, without mooring, with nothing to guide me. Now none of my relationships goes back more than thirty-five years.

If one day I come up against a new problem, unlike any that we discussed, with no memory of a response, and if she doesn't come to my assistance with her trove of solutions, her laugh, which heals all, and her marvelous humor, then I will know that Maco is never coming back. Never?

The idea that she's not there to help me face this unhappiness seems absurd. I search through our repertoire. . . . I create incredible chaos, I turn everything upside down, I mix everything up, love with lack of love, the past and the future, the present, which slips through my fingers, that neither she nor I could ever catch hold of, and I find nothing that evokes, even from afar, her death or mine and the way for the other to survive it.

We forgot about death.

She, who downplayed everything, even she couldn't have made light of this, couldn't have treated lightly the death of a young woman of thirty-five, pregnant, mother of two children, wife, daughter, beloved friend and sister. Impossible, isn't it?

It's serious this time, isn't it? As serious as possible. I avoid the word that I don't want to write, that I hate and that doesn't suit her.

Dead.

When I say the word, small windows open in my memory: "Died laughing, died of fright." Sometimes, referring to laughter or fear, she used that terrible word.

She laughed and at night was afraid of the slightest noise in the house. But she never used the terrible word on its own. Between laughter and fear, she never gave me the slightest hint.

How can I go on without you, Maco? I ask. In every encounter, it's you I look for.

I wait for everyone I meet to talk to me like she used to do. And I'm very disappointed when they don't know how. I bang up against others like a blind woman who bumps into a wall, a blind woman who searches for Maco everywhere.

No one will ever be like her. Who could be like a sister?

Wisdom consists of accepting people as they are, and not asking of them what they cannot give. Of not comparing the whole world to Maco. But I will never be wise.

The heart is a cake because life is supported by time.

"Time is on your side, you'll see, in time you'll forget." That's how someone close to me tried to console me.

I don't want to forget. I don't want time on my side. Time has taken away too many people I love for me to forget it.

Time is the enemy because its endlessness is responsible for all our misfortunes.

From the depths of sorrow, should I tell myself that I am nonetheless lucky? *Lucky.* I can't accept this word, not today and not tomorrow. Because sixty years of friendship would have been better than thirty-five, and no one will ever convince me otherwise. In the game of chance, Maco and I won the biggest prize, the most beautiful, and it seems difficult to continue alone after one has experienced the joy of loving each other. Difficult to play both parts. I know Maco so well that I can re-create her. I close my eyes, I see her, I hear her. But she cannot emerge from me. That's the difference now. She has entered into me. She is hidden somewhere inside me. She can't get out. She can't leave the film that is playing in my head. She will never get out again.

I will carry with me all my life the loss of Maco, like an illness, an amputation.

I can pinpoint the pain exactly. There, near my heart, it hurts, it pinches, it gnaws at me. I will miss her forever.

I want to believe in my childhood dreams when Maco and I spun the globe and, stretched out on the red-and-white-checked linoleum floor in our room overlooking the Atlantic Ocean, we told ourselves that somewhere, in America or France or Italy, which seemed so far from Fedala, now Mohammedia, and Casablanca, which remained Dar-el-Beida, we would find true love and friendship. We dreamed of the ideal friend and the most charming prince in the world. Who would they be?

Two princes, one for each of us, were enough. We knew we'd have lots of friends. False friends, true friends, traitors and faithful friends. One already senses these things at an early age in the school yard. We even forgot to include each other on the list of possible friends. We were too close, too near at hand; we were sisters! And isn't it a bit absurd to love your sister when you're six, ten, fourteen, or eighteen?

Now that Maco is gone, two chapters have closed. The one from childhood is closed forever. The little girl died. Mama lied to us. Another chapter is also closed, the one of unconditional friendship, so close to love. I've learned to be silent. I've learned to keep to myself everything I shared with her.

No more endless confessions; I will never again hear her advice, her problems, never again hear her hum "Your Song," never again will she wait for me at Nouasseur Airport, eager to show me her new hairdo, her new glasses, to prove to me that Casablanca isn't behind the times. . . .

I will never again be a sister.

I will never return to Ben m'sik cemetery. Even if they tell me that above her tombstone, early in the morning, so near the sea she loved, a dove and a white butterfly are flying over my sister, joyfully.

CHRISTINE ORBAN was born and raised in
Casablanca, Morocco. An award-winning equestrian,
she is the author of twelve novels, among them
the French national bestsellers *Fringues*
and *Le Silence des Hommes*. She lives in Paris
with her husband and two sons.

A B O U T   T H E   T Y P E

The text of this book was set in Janson,

a misnamed typeface designed in about 1690 by

Nicholas Kis, a Hungarian in Amsterdam. In 1919

the matrices became the property of the Stempel

Foundry in Frankfurt. It is an old-style book face of

excellent clarity and sharpness. Janson serifs are

concave and splayed; the contrast between

thick and thin strokes is marked.